OUT OF THE OOZE
THE STORY OF DR. TOM PRICE

Alexander Zaitchik

CONTENTS

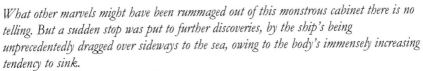

What other marvels might have been rummaged out of this monstrous cabinet there is no telling. But a sudden stop was put to further discoveries, by the ship's being unprecedentedly dragged over sideways to the sea, owing to the body's immensely increasing tendency to sink.
— Herman Melville, *Moby Dick*.

Chapter One
The Ultimate Soldier

On the morning of January 18, 2017, the senate opened hearings on the civic fitness of Thomas Edmunds Price, whom the incoming president had tapped to head the Department of Health and Human Services. With a trillion-dollar budget and portfolio of agencies touching the health of every American, HHS is the most consequential domestic post in government. The Price hearings had the added draw of showcasing a political paradox: The six-term Congressman had dedicated his career to undermining the very social programs that Donald Trump had promised, loudly and often, to protect during the campaign. Curiosity was high when Price's old friend and fellow Georgian, Johnny Isakson, kicked off the proceedings by introducing him as "the right man for the right job at the right time."

Then the rock was lifted on Tom Price, its bottom oozing with slime.

Six weeks had passed since Trump announced Price's nomination. Democrats used that time to comb through the congressman's dual record of far-right policymaking and dubious stock trading, identifying a curious pattern of their entwinement. For several hours, Price was confronted with the facts of this history, mostly evading and deflecting with the ease of a practiced and shameless operator. But his inquisitors did land clarifying body blows — clean hits that left Price dazed and wobbly under the television lights.

Minnesota's Al Franken landed one of these when he asked Price, a doctor long sworn to the Hippocratic Oath, about cigarettes.

Franken presented Price with a head-scratcher: Here was a man seeking a post defined by its engraved cornerstone-mandate to "protect the health of all Americans." And yet, this same man for decades owned stock in tobacco companies whose products kill nearly 500,000 Americans a year. Then there was the matter of Price's record opposing government regulation of the tobacco industry. Franken found this hard to square.

The exchange had a special salience given that both men had lost fathers to smoking-related illness. But the nominee did not feign regret over his stock holdings, or muster a piece of boilerplate about the dangers of smoking. The fact that he'd profited from the country's leading cause of preventable death was, said Price, an "interesting question and a curious observation."

The exchange with Franken framed the contrasts on display throughout the hearings. The Democratic senators subscribed to the view that has traditionally guided the HHS nominations of both parties: that the Department exists to improve the state of the nation's public and private health, to deliver the best care to the most people within the punishing limits of the private U.S. system — "especially," states the HHS mission, "those who are least able to help themselves."

Tom Price, on the other hand, views the health and sickness of Americans as a source of potential profit and nothing more. For him, health care is a consumer product, like a house or a boat, which people deserve in proportion to their ability to pay for it, and HHS should be administered according to this bedrock belief. The government should have no more of a role in providing care than it does in deciding the marketing tactics of Philip Morris (or in limiting the potential of politicians to profit from those tactics). Price's self-serving ideology explains his tobacco investments and everything else in a long record of opposing government public-health efforts. As catalogued in the *New England Journal of Medicine*, this record includes votes against the regulation of armor-piercing bullets and increased funding for mental health care, AIDS, malaria, tuberculosis, stem-cell, cancer, and other basic research projects.

It was perhaps inevitable that these politics would one day ascend the apex of HHS. Price, though a political freak in many ways, is a pure product of the defining and increasingly unstable contradiction at the heart of American health care: We have entrusted the production of the ultimate social good to a delivery system run by billion-dollar industries who embody the values and logic of shareholder capitalism.

The system has survived this contradiction for so long not because it works: It is as inefficient as it is inhumane. It has survived because of political force exerted over more than a century by the forces of organized medical reaction, one led for generations by doctor-businessmen like Tom Price.

* *

Price's political pedigree tracks to the rise of progressive agitation for universal health care at the turn of the twentieth-century.

Predating today's medical-industrial complex — before Big Pharma, Big Insurance, the sprawling device industry, the HMO chains — there were small-town doctors like Price's father and grandfather. They generally skewed conservative, entrepreneurs who hung shingles and enjoyed a unique status in their communities. Like other professions, they formed guilds to protect their interests.

"From the earliest days of their profession, physicians had organized their practices in the individualistic, fee-for-service, free-enterprise pattern; they had always been businessmen as well as public servants, and most wanted to keep it that way," writes the medical historian Monte M. Poen. "Even if the nation's medical rank and file had not been so imbued with individualistic precepts, [it] has been largely the well-to-do big-city specialists who have had the time and money to participate in medical politics."[1]

Tom Price fits the tradition of the reactionary "well-to-do big-city specialist." An orthopedic surgeon from Atlanta, Price began his political career as part of the American Medical Association's organized campaign against Hillary Care in 1993. Specifically, he was a speaker in the AMA's travelling lecture series, a time-honored tradition for healthcare reformers and their critics.

In the early 1900s, a coalition of social workers, union leaders, and reformers emerged who believed the U.S. should catch up with the social welfare policies of Europe. In the words of the influential reformer Edward Devine, it was time "to devote the fruits of abundance to the health of all,"

Organized medicine didn't think so. Neither did the nascent private insurance industry. Working with doctors groups, the Prudential Insurance Co. devised and funded a strategy to defeat the reform movement. At the center of this strategy was building a doctor's lecture circuit, on which Tom Price would cut his political teeth nine decades later. Prudential hired hundreds of doctors to tour churches and VFW halls and deliver terrifying warnings about the nightmare awaiting Americans on the other side of universal government insurance. They decried the labor-backed proposals as unnecessary, dangerous, and unconstitutional. With the outbreak of

---

[1] Price represents a narrower tradition of his medical specialty. As David Leonhardt noted in a column for the *New York Times*, orthopedic surgeons are the ultimate doctors of the one-percent: earning the industry's highest average salary of almost $450,000. Not bad money, but there's something about orthos that makes them think they deserve more. "Only 44 percent feel 'fairly compensated,' a smaller share than in almost every other specialty," writes Leonhardt.

"A lot of orthopedists aren't even happy being doctors. Just 49 percent say they would go into medicine if they had to make the decision again, compared with 64 percent of all doctors. Too many orthopedists are rich and think it's an injustice that they're not richer."

WWI, cradle-to-grave social insurance became "un-American" — an alien virus from the land of the Huns.

The popularity of the New Deal, followed by expanded health care during WWII, put the medical and insurance lobbies on their heels. The public overwhelmingly supported calls for folding wartime benefits into a permanent expansion of Social Security. But the enemies of reform quickly regrouped. The American Medical Association opened its first Washington office in 1943, from which it waged a sophisticated pushback operation in Congress, speaking halls, and the media. They were aided by the economic boom and anti-Communist hysteria of the early Cold War. The latter propelled the rise of groups like the Association of American Physicians and Surgeons, an archconservative group that echoed the fanatical anti-liberalism of the John Birch Society (and for years counted Tom Price as a member.)

The combined weight of medical and industry opposition defeated Harry Truman's hopes for universal insurance. "I have had some bitter disappointments as President," he wrote in his memoirs, "but the one that has troubled me most, in a personal way, has been the failure to defeat organized opposition to a national compulsory health-insurance program." Truman would find some measure of satisfaction shortly before his death, when LBJ traveled to his hometown of Independence, Missouri to sign the 1965 Medicare Act into law.

America's halting quest to achieve universal coverage was revived just as Tom Price solidified his professional and social position in the tony suburbs north of Atlanta. An accomplished orthopedic surgeon with a growing network of social and political connections, he was well poised to enter the ring when the Clinton administration announced the most significant healthcare plans since the Great Society reforms of the 1960s. Though the new reforms were moderate and "market-friendly," they sparked furious opposition by conservative think tanks, business groups, and medical associations. As the country debated the Clinton initiative, the AMA and its state affiliates cranked up the old lecture circuit and sent surrogates on the road. Tom Price barnstormed Georgia under the AMA banner, warning Americans against meddling with the current system.

"These [reforms] would limit the amount of care delivered and, probably, the quality of care given," Price said at the time.

Price soon learned to drop qualifiers like "probably" in his stump speeches and interviews. His political ambitions kindled, he grasped the value of blunter rhetorical instruments and argument. With this insight, Price began his journey to becoming the wealthiest and most-loathed director in the history of the Department of Health and Human Services.

* *

Chief among the barrier islands off Georgia's southern coast is a charmed little place called St. Simons. With its quaint downtown, plantation ruins, and perimeter of beach grass dunes sloping into the Atlantic, it is Martha's Vineyard with a history of Union Army occupation. On this isle sits a choice plot with a deed in Price's name.

We know about the property because it is listed in Price's financial disclosure statement. The plot, valued at up to $5 million, is one of many nest eggs Price has collected over the course of his long double-career as an entrepreneur and legislator. During his eight years in the Georgia senate and a dozen more in Congress, Price has amassed a personal fortune in excess of $12 million. In his official disclosure, his stock holdings alone filled 13 pages.

For most cabinet nominees, these numbers would generate shrugs. If dollars alone separated Price from the other two doctors nominated to HHS by Republican presidents — Otis Bowen and Louis Sullivan — nobody would much care. He is not the first millionaire to chair the Budget Committee, or run a federal department.

But there is a stink around Tom Price. A deep, unprecedented, flies abuzz stink. It appeared over him like a green fog on day one of his Senate hearings. It deepened over the course of questioning and followed him into his new office, where he guides policy shaping the future of Medicare, Medicaid, and the decisions of the Food and Drug Administration.

The stink around Tom Price is not dissipated by the lack of a rap sheet. Though never convicted of breaking Congressional rules or the U.S. criminal code, a body of circumstantial evidence strongly suggests he spent his career in Congress rubbing hard against both boundaries. While sitting on the Ways and Means Committee, Price enjoyed a brazen side hustle trading $300,000 worth of healthcare-related stocks, all the while advocating for many of these companies with colleagues and federal agencies.[2] In the restrained language of Oregon Democrat Ron Wyden, "When it comes to ethics, Tom Price falls well short of the standard the American people expect nominees to meet."

Exactly how far short, we may never know. The U.S. Attorney for the Southern District of New York, Preet Bharara, was reportedly investigating Price's dealings, and possibly planning an indictment, when President Trump fired him the day after the new HHS chief assumed office.

---

[2] Until he was forced to divest from more than 40 companies, Price's holdings included the full panoply of drug and medical device companies, including Pfizer, Eli Lilly and Bristol-Myers Squibb.

The problems with Tom Price go deeper than his suspicious stock trades. Those are surfacing methane bubbles that originate from deep fissures on the floor of a failed, inhumane, and corrupt healthcare system that Price embodies in caricature. The man with the Congressional nickname "Dr. No" has devoted his life to blocking all attempts to soften the edges of this system, then sharpening them further them on the backs of the poor, especially children and seniors. Despite the handful of human-sounding noises Price has learned to make over the years, his career amounts to a Creature Double-Feature of mutually reinforcing sadism and personal enrichment.

Tom Price likes to say that his worldview — anti-regulation, pro-market — is grounded in pragmatism and a desire, informed by personal experience, to improve patient "outcomes." His years as a surgeon, he likes to say, have taught him the centrality of what he piously calls the "sanctity of the patient-doctor relationship."

As will become clear in the following pages, this is a clumsy fig leaf in the form of a tattered *Saturday Evening Post* cover. Price publicly presents a Norman Rockwell dream world where government bureaucrats represent the only conceivable "outside force" in healthcare. Vanquished from this world are the profit-driven actors and market forces that in reality define U.S. healthcare: the risk-averse and corrupt HMOs, the care-shirking insurance companies, reckless and price-gouging drug makers. These actors also generate enormous wealth for a small number of Americans. Price is one of them. It has been his unique role to benefit from them in private, while in public banishing them behind curtains patterned with homilies about the sealed environment of the kindly family doctor's office.

The following survey pulls back the curtains on this racket. It confirms what critics of private healthcare have been saying for a century: that when Price and his ilk exalt the "sanctity" of the patient-doctor relationship, they mean the sanctity of private contracts. They mean the holy right of business, from the podiatry guild to the biggest drug multinational, to reap maximum profits from individuals and government programs without the slightest threat of interference. Public funds should never be used toward social goods — except when they can be easily spun along the way into shareholder value.[3]

---

[3] A rundown of this philosophy as expressed in official positions can be found in "Care for the Vulnerable vs. Cash for the Powerful — Trump's Pick for HHS," posted on the website of the *New England Journal of Medicine* in December 2016. The piece, quoted by Senator Al Franken during Price's first confirmation hearing, reviews the many anti-science, anti-public health positions that Price has held during his career.

Tom Price is famed on the right for being the perfect soldier. He is the system's true-believing T-1000 model, renowned for his cyborg-like dedication to the economic and political interests of his industry sponsors and allies. "Tom's like a machine," one former colleague told the *Atlanta Journal-Constitution* after Price's HHS nomination. Price is happy to confirm the reputation. "I'm one of those boring guys [without hobbies] whose work is his fun," he once said.

To glimpse Tom Price having fun, visit his office early. There you'll find him up with the sun, eyes steady behind rimless glasses crowned high with a receding puff of once-blonde hair. Perhaps you'll find him engaged in his career-defining crusade to crush the State Children's Health Insurance Program. Maybe he'll be micromanaging a governor's application to turn Medicaid into a block grant program with work requirements and co-pays, shutting millions out of coverage. Or maybe he'll be playing the ponies in the sector known as "Health Care Equipment and Services," placing buys with his Morgan Stanley broker in his serial-killer's voice that resides unnervingly equidistant between George Bush Sr. and Mister Rogers.

Whatever he's doing, he'll be doing it as a living monument to this country's shameful failure to care for its people. This is a political dereliction. It is also an indictment of market economics, though it looks like a success from the vantage of Health Care Equipment and Services, whose companies Price's aides are rumored to call "constituents." For them, and for their ultimate soldier, the current system is not a failure, but a golden goose requiring fierce protection from the ideological bird flu of alternative systems.

"There is no silver bullet, [no] one-size-fits-all solution for a nation so large and diverse," Price has said.

Except that there is. It's called single-payer universal healthcare. Keeping this fact out of politics for a century has required the coordinated vigilance of people like Tom Price. There's really nothing new or special about Donald Trump's HHS Secretary, save for the power of his current post. He is the latest in a long line of Tom Prices, just dirtier, more diligent and more focused than most. Whatever he achieves at HHS, he's more than earned his retirement on the beaches of St. Simon.

Chapter Two
A Greed Grows in Georgia

Tom Price was born in Lansing, Michigan, in 1954. The son and grandson of doctors, he followed the family line and attended medical school at the University of Michigan. After completing his coursework in 1979, he relocated to Atlanta and entered a residency in orthopedic surgery at Emory University. There he met a young anesthesiologist named Elizabeth whom he would shortly marry. Like Tom, "Betty" held conservative views and liked the Atlanta area.

In 1983, the young couple moved to Roswell, an upscale suburb thirty minutes north of the city. Here, among the town's leafy grid, a young and thinly mustachioed Tom Price began his journey to the pinnacle of U.S. healthcare policy.

Each morning, he and Betty commuted to the Grady Memorial Hospital in downtown Atlanta, where Price would one day direct the orthopedic clinic. They nurtured roots in their adopted state by joining a range of civic, professional, and social groups. Decades later, in Washington, Price would proudly note his 17 years of perfect attendance as a member of the Roswell Rotary Club.

In the mid-1980s, Tom founded a private practice, Compass Orthopedics. The business grew and grew, and a decade later merged with Georgia's largest outpatient network of orthopedic care, a multi-million dollar company called Resurgens Orthopedics. After the merger, Price served as Resurgens' chairman of the board, not long after the firm settled a huge Medicare fraud suit (more about that below). The firm's growth provided the basis for the voluminous real estate and stock market portfolio that would make Price one of the wealthiest members of the House of Representatives.

As described in the previous chapter, Price began to raise his public profile in 1993 as a bit player in the national AMA effort to derail the Clinton health care reforms. By all accounts, Price proved an effective foot soldier in the fight.

When the GOP stormed the U.S. House of Representatives the following year, he had established a reputation among Peachtree State Republicans. His ambitions were kindled by the power achieved by his fellow Georgian, Newt Gingrich. Like Price, the new House Speaker had moved to the state to study at Emory, and settled in one of the state's most conservative suburban belts. Price was better acquainted with another Georgia Republican, Bob Barr, whose Congressional district abutted Gingrich's. When Barr formed a state task force on Medicare in 1995, he brought Price into his brain trust. That same year, the state senator representing Price's home district called him to say she was retiring. Was the doctor interested in running for her seat?

He was.

In 1996, at the age of 41, Price ran successfully as a "consensus builder" to represent Georgia's 56th district, a stretch of tony bedroom communities connecting Cherokee, Gwinnett, and North Fulton counties. Downplaying his support for the kind of flame-throwing conservatism that defined 1994's "Republic Revolution," he ran as a practical Republican: A problem-solving doctor you could trust to get things done for the common good.

Previewing a line he would deliver hundreds of times in the coming years, he told the *Atlanta Journal-Constitution*, "My education promotes a common-sense approach to problems. It encourages evaluating symptoms, identifying problems, and charting a course of action."

Though ascendant in Washington, Republicans were embattled in Atlanta. Price arrived at the state house to find a minority GOP caucus without much enthusiasm or much of a plan. Few proved so eager to change the party's position as Price. He soon built a reputation as a tireless if stiff party strategist and tactician. For his work ethic and intelligence, he was twice nominated minority whip. But he never won any popularity awards. An investigative review of Price's statehouse years by the *Journal-Constitution* reveals a man cold to the touch, a Michigan native who never really thawed under the Georgia sun. Former staff and colleagues remember Price as calculating and indefatigable, a quick-tempered know-it-all consumed with detail and control. It is a picture at odds with Price's later claims of ignorance regarding large stock trades made on his behalf during his years in Congress.

For eight years, Price served as Georgia's most dedicated vector for right wing health care messaging and legislation, and Medicaid in particular. He was reliably conservative on every other issue — from gay marriage to criminal justice to the Georgia state flag — but his central passion was undermining public assistance programs from his perch on the Health and Human Services committee.[4] His work promised to hurt more people than

---

[4] On rare occasions, Price worked with Democrats on symbolic bills that likely raised eyebrows in Roswell. In 2000, he co-sponsored a Democratic bill proclaiming a "Great American Meatout Day." The bill recognized "a wholesome plant based diet...reduces the risk of heart disease [and] helps preserve our forests, grasslands, and other wildlife habitats and reduces

it might have in other parts of the country: Then and now, nearly one in seven Georgia residents have no coverage, putting the state near the bottom of the 50 states.

Price made his first stand in favor of this status quo in 1998, when Georgia Governor Zell Miller tried to expand Medicaid access for 300,000 children living near the poverty line. Price led the resistance, fighting tooth and nail to stop an expansion of the State Children's Health Insurance Program, or SCHIP. Some of Price's fellow Republicans refused to join him. They admitted a crisis in Georgia healthcare and noted that Washington provided most of the money. Price was unmoved, refusing to admit that uninsured children were a problem.

"I know of no study that shows these individuals have no access," Price told the *Journal-Constitution*. "Uninsured children already are treated by doctors and hospitals."

This was an ice blooded and intellectually obtuse half-truth. Uninsured poor children receive emergency care across the country. But you don't have to be a doctor to know the difference between healthcare and an ER room. The way Price chose to elide the issue chafed against his preferred rationale for so-called tort reform. During his state senate career, Price was a steady and fierce advocate for limiting malpractice awards. In making his case, he often stood on feigned concern for the fiscal health of small and rural hospitals. These institutions, he said, were threatened by large single-plaintiff lawsuits and class-action settlements. But the biggest burden faced by these hospitals was the growing use of emergency care by the uninsured — a crisis SCHIP expansion was designed to alleviate.

Five years after going to the mat against Zeller's SCHIP expansion — a fight he ultimately lost — Price made a stand on his other pet issue: limiting medical malpractice settlements. As with most of the positions that define his career, Price was a local grunt in a national campaign coordinated far above his station. Echoing bills then appearing in Washington and around the country, Price submitted legislation to cap malpractice awards at $250,000 for individuals, and $750,000 for class action suits. The caps were necessary, Price said, to rein in the "unrestrained escalation of [jury] awards . . . that are out of control."

Despite Price's insistence otherwise, no studies had found a link between such caps and reductions in premiums. Nor did settlements rival emergency room traffic as a stress multiplier on small and rural hospitals. The caps would, however, be a gift to doctor's groups, the pharmaceutical industry, and the makers of medical equipment. With caps in place, these groups would be freed from all accountability. Even when they caused

pollution of our waterways by soil particles, debris, manure, and pesticides."

widespread pain and suffering — be it through carelessness or intentionally taking risks to turn a profit — they would be shielded from their victims' pursuit of justice through the courts.

At the time Price submitted his bill, the health industry accounted for 16 of Price's top 20 campaign contributors. But they weren't necessarily asking for original thinking from their rising star in Georgia. It was enough that he forwarded the mission and copied the legislation crafted by his minders at the corporate-funded American Legislative Exchange Council, or ALEC. It was ALEC that nurtured Price as a state senator, creating ties that deepened throughout his years in Congress, and that he brings with him to HHS.

ALEC

* *

ALEC was founded in 1973 to increase corporate influence at the state level. Unlike groups with similar-sounding names, such as the National Council of State Legislatures, corporate money has always been at the center of ALEC's operations and purpose. By teaming state lawmakers with corporations in various task forces, the group seeks to harmonize lawmakers' efforts with the priorities of its corporate members, whose dues make up the bulk of its operating budget. It has succeeded all expectations. ALEC is a now a well-oiled bill factory whose legislative products routinely appear in statehouses across the 50 states. As more of its alumni have moved into powerful federal positions, ALEC has developed a program to keep its alumni and younger members communication.

Tom Price is a shining example of ALEC's corporate assembly line: from task force member to "Federal Relations" mentor. But he is hardly the first. When Price joined ALEC in the mid-1990s, the group had a record of success in furthering corporate and rightwing agendas from gun law to energy policy and everything in between.

must be more than 20%

"With our success rate at more than 20 percent [of bills passed] I would say that ALEC is a good investment," then-executive director Samuel Brunelli told corporate backers in 1995. "Nowhere else can you get a return that high."

When Price joined ALEC's task force on health care, he was continuing a Georgia tradition. In the early 1990s, Georgia state senator Tom Wilder co-chaired the committee during the pushback against Clinton's reform agenda. Today, the task force is co-chaired by Georgia state senator Judson Hill. Both men were paired with corporate co-chairs with much to gain by the passage of tort caps and the ascension of Tom Price to the agency controlling the FDA. Wilder's corporate co-chair, Syntex Labs, settled what the FDA called "a landmark case" involving misleading advertising. Not to be outdone, Hill's co-chair, Takeda Pharmaceuticals U.S.A., recently paid out one of the largest drug settlements in history — $2.37 billion on thousands of claims it purposely hid the cancer risks of its products.

ALEC's agenda found clean reflection in Tom Price's legislative priorities in the Georgia senate: stopping Medicaid expansion, capping malpractice settlements, and reducing regulatory oversight and enforcement. Indeed, every piece of Tom Price's agenda as a state senator and Congressman first appeared as a model bill under ALEC letterhead: from private Medicare and Medicaid accounts that would reduce coverage, to the elimination of non-federally mandated benefits. More recently, ALEC has been a major force in coordinating state-level efforts to oppose and repeal the Affordable Care Act. As we will see, Price did not sever his relationship with ALEC upon his election to Congress, but helped pioneer a new model for alumni involvement

* *

In 2003, Price was 49 years old and ready for his turn on the national stage. After he announced his candidacy for Georgia's Sixth, most observers had him as a favorite. The seat once held by Newt Gingrich (who did not endorse Price) was the country's second-wealthiest Republican seat. In every respect, it looked a lot like the district that sent him to the Georgia senate.

Some things had changed since his first race in 1996. Price was now much richer than the well-off people he was running to represent. He now owned millions worth of stock and real estate. His private practice had been absorbed into a sprawling $50 million-a-year outpatient network with nearly 500 employees, for which he served as a partner and founding board member. That company, Resurgens, would become his biggest donor in Congress.[5] In the mid-90s, shortly before Price joined its board, it had also become the subject of a multi-million-dollar Medicare fraud suit.[6]

Price has never commented on his company's fraud settlement. But

---

[5] When Price left Congress to join Trump's cabinet, the company topped his list of his career donors with $220,335 in contributions.

[6] The week of Price's HHS confirmation hearings, *Mother Jones* reported the details of a lawsuit filed against the company's surgery center by a whistleblower under the False Claims Act. The whistleblower alleged that the center and its staff anesthesiologists submitted fraudulent bills to Medicare and Medicaid as part of a systematic kickback scheme between 1993 and 1997. All told, the company and its employees settled for nearly $5 million.

there is no reason to think it should trouble him. Doctors gaming public assistance programs does not upset Price. He gets angry when the feds and the courts call doctors and medical businesses to account for their corruption and criminal conduct. This finds institutional expression in Price's membership to the Association of Physicians and Surgeons, whose opposition to regulation is so extreme it makes the AMA look like the Physicians for a National Health Program.

The details of the Resurgens settlement didn't hurt Price's standing with donors and the voters of the Georgia's Sixth. Price raised more than $1 million for the campaign, mostly from a familiar list of doctor's groups and medical companies, and cruised to victory with speeches about the country's "broken" tax and healthcare systems. His solution to the former was to scrap the income tax, capital gains, and the IRS. His fix for the latter was a laundry list of clichés about putting "patients in charge" and capping malpractice settlements. He sold both on the strength of his "surgeon's mentality." But if Tom Price's politics is akin to surgery, it is surgery employed without anesthesia, and one most Americans can't afford.

Over the next 12 years, Price would place himself at the center of Congressional efforts to gut Medicare and Medicaid, the programs that provide a modicum of security to the most vulnerable Americans. He would do this as a studious freshman, as a not very convincing "Tea Party" Republican, as the strategist-chair of the Republican Study Committee, and as the Chair of the House Budget Committee.

When he arrived in Washington, the future face of opposition to the Affordable Care Act was still wearing his mustache.

Chapter Three
The Honorable "Dr. No"

In early 2005, at the start of the 109th Congress, Tom Price delivered his first speech on the House floor. As he would many times, the rookie Congressman addressed a nearly empty chamber. His subject was the looming collapse of Social Security, Medicare and Medicaid. Barring drastic reforms, he declared, these programs were headed toward the same fiscal cliff. The first House resolution bearing Price's name soon followed, a statement on the need "to move the Nation's current health care delivery system toward a defined contribution system."

The speech and its twin resolution set the tone for Price's six terms in Congress —brash policy delivered in subdued tones that often bordered on pathetic. Never one for crowds, with the charisma of a bowl of pudding, Price was content with the lazy attentions of late night C-SPAN cameras and the future readership of the Congressional Record. In his approach to media, Price differed from his outspoken predecessor from Georgia's sixth, Newt Gingrich. But Price shared with Gingrich a desire to be taken serious as a heavyweight policy intellect that pushed hardline policies beyond consensus boundaries. With a strengthened Republican majority behind a reelected Republican President, it seemed like an auspicious moment for Price to do just this. He arrived in Washington eager to make his mark and keep climbing.

"I remember [it] clear as a bell," Price's former campaign manager, Jared Thomas, told the *Journal-Constitution*. "In August 2004 right after he won the seat, he said that he thought he had a good dozen years in the House but he wanted to be considered for health secretary or surgeon general."

Price began in Congress as he did in Georgia — in the minority opposition. Price didn't factor much in the major healthcare policy event of his first term, Bush's expansion of Medicare drug coverage known as Part D. But following the 2006 midterms that saw Democrats retake Congress, Price emerged as the leader of an informal House GOP group that called itself the "Official Truth Squad." A kind of extracurricular club for young GOP back benchers, the Truth Squad became fixtures on late night C-SPAN. They would stay in the House chamber after everyone else had left and trade tepid insults and talking points with Democrats late into the night. After a year of this, the *Weekly Standard* urged Price and his friends to stop, dismissing their club as emblematic of Washington's "cavernous abyss" of grandstanding and dysfunction.

"They do not 'dialogue' with each other," commented the magazine. "They address only themselves — and the insomniacs and junkies who watch C-SPAN at 11 p.m."

The after-hours shenanigans did endear him to the party's leadership. After one term he was chosen as a deputy to Minority Whip Roy Blunt of Missouri.

Price quickly established one of the most conservative records in Congress,[7] voting the hardline on immigration, fiscal and social issues. In 2007, he sponsored the "Common Sense English Act" to amend the Civil Rights Act so that employers could fire employees who did not speak English.

His future, however, was not in becoming another Tom Tancredo, the Colorado representative who made his name on the immigration issue. Tom Price would stake his future on the privatization of health care and assaults on public assistance. His emergence as the Tancredo of health care is a tale told in the major legislative efforts of his second term, a crucial period during which he emerged as a party leader and gained the Congressional nickname "Dr. No."

In January of 2007, Price made a stand against one of the greatest symbols of waste and corruption in the U.S. healthcare system: the absurdly high cost of drugs compared to countries where the government negotiates costs.

In a 255-170 vote, Congress passed a bill allowing the secretary of Health and Human Services to negotiate prices with drug companies. This would leverage the government's bargaining power achieved through its representation of more than 40 million Medicare recipients. The White House, Tom Price, and most Republicans opposed the bill as "government meddling," claiming, against all logic and evidence, that it would lead to higher drug costs.

Price assailed the bill on the grounds of familiar standbys: patient choice and the public's sacred right to get fleeced by the pharmaceutical companies. The bill was, he said, "a solution in search of a problem. The Democrats think that Washington can make better decisions than the American people about very personal medical matters."

Price also claimed a concern for drug safety and a sudden awareness of the moral hazard posed by the profit motive. "Washington bureaucrats will decide which drugs will be available for patients, not from a scientific or

---

[7] In what would be a rare instance of dissent from his party's leadership, Price was one of 18 GOP dissenters against the vote to reauthorize the Patriot Act without a sunset clause.

safety standpoint but purely based upon money," he said. "That's not the way we ought to be making health care decisions; those decisions ought to be made by patients and doctors."

In June, Price followed up this performance by sponsoring a health system overhaul that looked like an ALEC wish list: it spanned tort reform, tax credits, and personalized accounts. Though the bill went nowhere, the Empowering Patients First Act would grow from its embryo, appearing years later as Price's perennial replacement for the Affordable Care Act.

Nobody could have anticipated that at this at the time. More pressing from the GOP's perspective was a looming fight to stop another Democratic expansion of the State Children's Health Insurance Program.

In October of 2007, George W. Bush vetoed a $35 billion five-year expansion of SCHIP to help poor children across the country. Even as the White House authorized more than $150 billion on the occupation of Iraq in that year alone, the President blasted the legislation. "What you're seeing when you expand eligibility for federal programs is the desire by some in Washington, D.C., to federalize health care," said Bush of the SCHIP expansion bill.

Naturally, Price supported the veto. It was immaterial that Georgia would be hardest hit by the failure to reauthorize SCHIP the following year. Georgia's Republican Governor, Sonny Perdue, supported the expansion, which would have kept the state's PeachCare for Kids program running for five years with an additional $1 billion. The program was aimed at those who didn't qualify for Medicaid, but also could not afford the price of a "patient-doctor" relationship. PeachCare for Kids covered more than a quarter-million Georgian children.

Price, representing the wealthiest district in the state, described the SCHIP spending not as an attempt to cover these children, but as "a cynical attempt to score political points. President Bush was correct to veto the bill."

Just a few months later, in February of 2008, Price was suddenly much less concerned about government spending, and he voted to amend Social Security to allow for increased Medicare payouts to doctors.

* *

By the event of Barack Obama's election in November of 2009, Price had fully shed his junior status. He was 54 years old and considered a policy guru within the party. That party now faced a generational challenge in the form of a Democratic White House and Congress determined to introduce an historic health care bill.

Price greeted the Obama era in the 111th Congress by introducing a bill of his own, called the "More Choices, More Children Act." Though he described it as sharing the same goals of SCHIP expansion, i.e., insuring more children, the bill would have insured fewer kids, and adding new restrictions such as requiring proof of citizenship.

Price understood the ground was shifting. With Obama's election, conservative think tanks began organizing events to challenge the new Democratic president. The events featured old strains of paranoia and extremism not seen in decades. Price, a member of the conservative caucus, was drawn to these flames, even if he hated crowds. He became an early and familiar face at tea party events around the Capitol and back home in Georgia, awkwardly embracing the Gadsden flag.

At live events and on cable television, Price became a common voice against Democratic reforms. This included the so-called "public option," which Price called "the most underappreciated and dangerously impactful idea being debated" within the larger health care discussion. A government insurance plan, he said, was "simply a backdoor path to a government takeover of health care." Once again, he pretended as if "the bottom line" only concerned the government, and not privately run insurance companies and HMOs. "The government views care in terms of dollars and cents rather than patients and their doctors [and] medical decisions are always made with a focus on the bottom line, rather than the patient's best interest. I have seen first-hand how government-run programs ration, delay and deny care."

In hundreds of TV hits and op-eds, Price cited the VA, Medicare, Medicaid, and the Indian Health Service as examples of failed government-run providers. Aside from not being failed programs, it was a false dichotomy: Most of the people using these programs did not face a choice between them and private coverage, but between them and *no coverage at all.* Shibboleths about "access" obscured this truth only clumsily. Ditto his many arguments in defense of "ownership," "tax credits," and "private accounts." It all added up to statements combining mendacity with illogic, such as this classic Tom Price doozy: "When it makes financial sense for all Americans to be covered, the uninsured will disappear."

Price's industry backers and allies found such gems worthy of largesse. Of nearly $800,000 Price raised for his 2010 re-election, nearly all came from various sectors of medical and pharmaceutical industries.

They got their money's worth in the run-up to the health care vote of November 2009. Price, it seemed, was everywhere: at podiums on the Capitol lawn, leading chants of "Kill the bill!", on the radio discussing the "sanctity of the doctor-patient relationship," on Fox News talking about rationing and the horrors of socialized medicine. In a video interview with the far-right Association of American Physicians and Surgeons, he adlibbed what sounded like a public service announcement from 1955. "Make sure that you're in the game," he urged his fellow doctors. "This is for all the marbles."

In Congress, too, Price had found his voice. The usually mild-mannered doctor could be heard at uncharacteristic volume on the Saturday morning of November 7, 2009, when the House began debating the health care bill. *Think Progress* reported the scene: "As the Democratic Women's Caucus took to the microphone on the House floor to offer their arguments for how the bill would benefit women, House Republicans — led by Rep. Tom Price (R-GA) — repeatedly talked over, screamed, and shouted objections. 'I object, I object, I object, I object, I object,' Price interjected as Rep. Lois Capps (D-CA) tried to hold the floor."

According to the *Journal-Constitution*, Price "interjected calls for 'parliamentary inquiry,' questioning everything and anything taking place on the U.S. House floor."

When the Affordable Care Act became law, Price moved "from resistance to repeal." He accrued power as he did so, joining the powerful Ways and Means Committee, whose portfolio covers Social Security and Medicare, and becoming chairman of the conservative House Republican Study Committee. He wielded his new power and profile with a reworked version of his Bush-era health care overhaul, rechristened as the Empowering Patients First Act.

In July of 2010, Price became one of the 30 inaugural members of the Tea Party caucus. Reflecting that group's disturbing reclamation of "states rights" rhetoric, Price helped launch a "10th Amendment Task Force" in Congress.

As part of reinventing himself as a Tea Party firebrand, Price sounded the most audacious rhetoric of his public career. "The tide of soft tyranny must be turned back if we hope to remain both the land of the free and a land of opportunity," he said in announcing the 10th Amendment task force. At a rally in Atlanta, he invoked Sam Adams and urged the audience to "set brush fires for freedom."

* *

Following the passage of the ACA, Price did more than submit his alternative bill in a perennial symbolic act of defiance. He also led his party's effort to hack away at the edges of the new law. He went after the employer mandate, an advisory panel on restraining Medicare spending, limits on administrative costs in the insurance industry, and revenue-generating taxes on medical devices.

His biggest push found him teaming up with Paul Ryan to turn Medicaid into lump sum block grants, which would have cost his home state of Georgia nearly $50 billion in federal funding and cut health care for thousands. According to the *Journal-Constitution*, a Kaiser study conducted after the passage of the ACA showed "block grants would hurt hospitals, especially those already losing money caring for the poor and uninsured." This included the downtown Atlanta hospital where Tom and Betty Price began their careers, Grady Memorial.

For his effort in opposition, Price continued climbing up the party hierarchy with prestigious if not headline-making appointments. In 2011, Price was elected chair of the Republican Policy Committee. This position, the party's fifth highest in Congress, was as far as Tom Price would go.

$$* *$$

When Price began his fourth term in 2012, there were rumors he was planning a senate run. He never did. Instead, he stayed busy in the House: voting for government shutdowns, introducing his "Empower" replacement bill, fighting off attempts to monitor Medicare fraud and abuse in senior care, trying to prevent disabled workers from collecting earned unemployment and SSDI benefits at the same time. In his spare moments, he raised money for his easy reelections and managed a growing private fortune.

In January of 2015, Price followed Paul Ryan as chair of the Budget Committee. With a Republican-controlled senate, he was in the best position of his career to shape national policy. And everyone knew it. At the Heritage Foundation, on the cusp of his ascension, Price was introduced as "the tip of the spear." In his talk that followed, Price promised not to waste his new powers, but use them to "normalize controversial approaches" to popular programs. He really did think they were popular, he said, because Mitt Romney ticket had won the senior vote in 2012.

He ended with a promise about his forthcoming budget: "The president is going to be laid bare," he said. "[It will prove] the emperor has no clothes."

Upon its release, that budget won plaudits from the right for being balanced on the backs of the poor. The bill that left his Committee — "A Balanced Budget for a Stronger America" — cut $5.5 trillion mostly by looting the coffers of social programs, while adding new defense spending.

Then, a bolt from the blue: Donald Trump was elected President. Like Price, Trump wanted to repeal the ACA. Unlike Price, he campaigned on promises not to touch Social Security and Medicare. Though hardly a match made in heaven, Price must have liked his chances for a cabinet position. Sure enough, he received an invitation to Trump Tower just a week after the election. A week after the meeting, Trump formally announced Price as his nominee to head Health and Human Services. Price must have wondered what ghosts from his past would appear during the hearings scheduled to begin in January, two days before Inauguration.

Chapter Four
Secretary of Sadism

B etween the November announcement of his nomination and his February confirmation, Tom Price starred in a political version of *This is Your Life*. Friends and allies spanning the fullness of his career chimed in with hosannas: The Medical Association of Georgia, the Association of American Physicians and Surgeons, Resurgens Orthopedics, the Republican Study Committee — the whole gang was there.

The American Legislative Exchange Council issued the most effusive statements. In a long letter that somehow omitted the fact of Price's former membership, the group celebrated Price as "a fierce advocate of returning the authority to states [and] a life-long champion of market-based reforms." There is, ALEC concluded, "no one with more experience to enact meaningful healthcare reform."[8]

Since the group's founding in 1973, ALEC had groomed a number of state senators for influential national careers. But rarely had one been as perfectly placed to realize so much of the group's agenda at such a key moment. With Republicans in control of Congress and the White House, the HHS secretary would be at the center of the GOP's long-planned multi-front assault on landmark Democratic reforms — from drafting and passing an ACA replacement, to pushing drastic changes to the way states fund and implement Medicaid.

HHS is one of the most powerful fiefs in the federal government. Its lineage dates to the 1953 creation of the Department of Health, Education and Welfare under Dwight Eisenhower. A quarter-century later, under Jimmy Carter, Education was split off, creating the modern department. The HHS mission statement reflects the department's central responsibility of administering Medicare and Medicaid. It calls for "protecting the health of all Americans and providing essential human services, especially for

---

[8] Throughout his years in Congress, Price had remained an active alumnus and mentor to the ALEC community. As recently as March of 2016, he joined an ALEC conference call with state-level members on the subject of "free market solutions to federal budget challenges."

those who are least able to help themselves." To accomplish this, the department wields a trillion-dollar budget and oversees a sprawling bureaucracy of nearly 80,000 employees in satellite offices across the country, anchored by a granite mother ship across from Bartholdi Park and within sight of the Capitol dome. Along with the Centers for Medicare and Medicaid Services, its purview covers a dozen key agencies including the Centers for Disease Control and Prevention, the Food and Drug Administration, and the National Institutes of Health.

As the head of HHS, Price would wield a power so enormous it is the stuff of political fantasy. But first, he had to be confirmed. The televised hearings would put Price under a national microscope for the first time. The result was a uniquely disturbing picture of American democracy at work.

* *

It was grey and chilly on the January morning Price sat before the Senate Committee on Health, Education, Labor, and Pensions. After his old pal Johnny Isakson introduced him as "the right man at the right time," Price delivered an opening statement defined by familiar themes and a shamelessness that would make a used car salesman blush.

"Anyone who has ever treated a child knows how fulfilling it is to look into the eyes of a parent and tell them our team has helped heal their son or daughter — to give them peace of mind," Price said.

It was a remarkable stab at sentimentalism from a man who has built a career out of fighting efforts to provide poor children with health care. He next spoke of his reluctant entry into public life, driven by his desire to "help solve the issues harming the delivery of medicine."

Price spent the rest of the day ducking and weaving around the efforts of Democratic senators to understand the red flags that decorated his long record.

When Vermont's Bernie Sanders asked Price his thoughts on Trump's election promises to protect Medicare and negotiate drug costs, Price demurred. When Minnesota's Al Franken asked him about his decades of tobacco holdings, and his vote against giving FDA power to regulate tobacco, Price called it a "curious observation" and mumbled about the nature of mutual funds.

The most consistent line of questioning concerned Price's recent purchases of stock in two health care companies: Innate Immunotherapeutics and Zimmer Biomet. Price had twice intervened with regulatory bodies on behalf of the companies, raising questions about double-dealing. When pressed to explain his actions, Price blamed his stockbroker. "I wasn't making those decisions," he told Elizabeth Warren of Massachusetts. "I'm offended by the insinuation, senator." (Details of these transactions are below.)

The following week, Price faced a second round of hearings before the Senate Finance Committee.

Ron Wyden, the committee's ranking Democrat, said point-blank that he didn't see patients at the center of Tom Price's healthcare philosophy. "I see money, and I see special interests," he told a stone-faced Price. Later, in a testy exchange with New Jersey's Bob Menendez, Price attempted to wiggle loose from his entire record in public life. His work as a legislator, Price maintained, was "not necessarily the work I would promote" as Secretary.

Then there was the swirl of controversy still trailing Price from the first hearing. The night before his second hearing, Finance committee staff distributed a memo regarding Price's financial disclosures and tax history. The itemized memo included a laundry list of ethically dubious acts, non-disclosures and indiscretions, including the gross undervaluing by half of his stock in Innate Immunotherapeutics, an Australian pharmaceutical company. (See the next chapter.)

In the end, Price was confirmed, but not in the usual way. Democrats boycotted the vote — as they did for Trump's choices for Treasury and the EPA — forcing his fellow Republicans on the Finance Committee to suspend rules and vote without them. On a vote of 14-0, Price's nomination was sent to the senate and approved by the GOP majority.

On February 3, Price officially vacated his House seat and assumed control of HHS. He did so just as his erstwhile colleagues were preparing a push to make his old ACA replacement bill the law of the land.

* *

It soon turned out that the GOP's faith in Tom Price and his bill was misplaced. The health care overhaul Price had long championed went down in embarrassing defeat a month after he was sworn in. As of this writing, TrumpCare lives on, but the political calculus underlying it appears to be faulty at its core.

But repeal-and-replace is not the only way Price and the Republicans can undo the ACA's core reforms. As HHS chief, Price has the power to make important changes to the law and its enforcement. The HHS interim boss put some of these into effect before Price's confirmation, including cuts to the ACA's enrollment period and minimum standards of coverage. Trump's HHS also didn't wait for Price before slashing the ACA's marketing budget, a move credited with impacting enrollment downward.

Price has a large toolbox at HHS for monkey wrenching the ACA and other reforms. He can withdraw his department's support for lawsuits involving the ACA. He can work with the White House to "exempt"-ify the individual mandate out of existence. He can assist the conservative crusade against Planned Parenthood and the ACA's public funding of contraceptives. (Price can also use his position to further an anti-gay agenda through the HHS' Office of Civil Rights. His deputy at that post, Roger Severino, has a long record of making anti-gay comments.)

At the center of these policy controls are the Centers for Medicare and Medicaid Services, or CMS. With its power over the health care of one-third of all Americans, CMS is the jewel in the HHS crown. As a Congressman, Price dealt with the agency as a supplicant. Now he controls it, in collaboration with a likeminded CMS administrator who does his bidding.

Among the policy levers under Price's control is CMS' power to shape the future of Medicaid. CMS has the authority to approve "waivers" that grant states the right to diverge from federal rules. These applications come from the states, 32 of which were under Republican control following the 2016 election. With Price at HHS, these states can transform how Medicaid works for millions of Americans and in a number of awful ways. Waivers can, for example, let states implement private accounts and mandate work requirements.

The most important position under HHS Secretary, then, is CMS Director. On March 2, Trump nominated to the position a health industry executive named Seema Verma. Unknown to most Americans, Verma has long been a minor celebrity in conservative policy circles.

A first-generation Indian-American, Verma worked in various federal agencies before founding a health-policy consulting firm in 2001. As Founder and CEO of SVC Incorporated, she worked with governors of both parties to help implement the Affordable Care Act. But her work with conservative lawmakers in Indiana and other states made her a star on the right. To be specific, her deft use of a Medicaid regulation known as Section 1115. This bylaw allows states to pursue experiments for administering Medicaid and CHIP known as "Research & Demonstration Projects." Doing so required only the review and green light of CMS. According to the law, any proposal can be considered, so long as it promises better or similar care at lower cost.

Under Obama, CMS rejected most waiver applications and stalled some others. Of dozens of submitted proposals, six were approved. Of the six, Seema Verma's Indiana application went the furthest in advancing policy goals, though Obama's CMS vetoed its work requirements.

Verma's "Healthy Indiana Plan," passed by the state in 2008, mandated savings accounts and higher deductibles for Medicaid recipients. These "reforms" were matched with a harsh punitive mechanism: a two-month failure to contribute to the private accounts resulted in a penalty of losing coverage for one year.

At the time, she described its structure as an attempt to meld "two themes of American society that typically collide in our health-care system, rugged individualism and the Judeo-Christian ethic.... HIP combines these diametrically opposed themes by promoting personal responsibility while providing subsidized health protection to those who can least afford it."

After the passage of the ACA in 2010, she designed a waiver application to tailor Indiana's newly mandated expansion of Medicaid. Obama's HHS approved most of the application with minor tweaks. The result was known as HIP 2.0. It included private accounts and lock-out periods, reflecting Verma's belief that "able-bodied" Americans can make "rational decisions" that require "personal responsibility" even if their income barely exceeds the federal policy level.

Price wasted no time setting the stage for his future CMS administrator. Days after his confirmation, but still a month before Verma arrived, CMS acting administrator Patrick Conway proposed a raft of rule changes to state Medicaid requirements, including limiting enrollment periods and lowering minimum standards of coverage.

On March 13, the day Verma was confirmed by a vote of 55 to 43, Price signed two letters on HHS stationary announcing that the agency was open for a new kind of business. The first, sent to the nation's 50 governors, requested waiver submissions for deficit-neutral plans that "alleviate" the ACA's "burdens." The brief dispatch, carbon copied to Treasury Secretary Steve Mnuchin, expressed the Department's desire to assist states in drafting waivers and review their applications "on an expedited basis." It cited Alaska's creation of statewide high-risk pools as a model.

Price and Verma co-signed a second, longer letter to the same 50 governors. This communiqué expanded on the duo's vision for a "golden age" of "fast-tracked" Medicaid waivers and other state-level reforms. They described the ACA's mandated Medicaid expansion as "a clear departure from the core, historical mission of the program" because it increased funds for those living slightly above poverty. They encouraged governors to follow Verma's lead and add work requirements, and to prepare recipients for the private insurance market by making them pay monthly premiums and copays for emergency room visits.

In the language and priorities of the letters, Price once again was closely echoing an ALEC agenda written by corporations.

In the group's public statement celebrating Price's nomination, it heralded just these reforms. "For low-income Americans," ALEC stated, "allowing states to enact reform policies such as giving Medicaid recipients the option to opt-into a private, capitated health insurance plan paid for by the state will create a bridge to portable, private insurance that would bring more cost-consciousness when seeking their health plan."

Price and Verma's plans for state-level innovation are unmatched by enthusiasm for innovation at the national level. Price made this clear during his confirmation hearings when he attacked the Center for Medicare and Medicaid Innovation, created by the ACA to reduce Medicaid costs. Price rejected the very premise of the CMMI on grounds that it "carries the full force of the federal government. I simply reject that [Washington D.C.] is where decisions [about services, payment, and care] ought to be made."

* *

Like Tom Price, Verma has a history of mixing public business with private profit. According to an investigation by *USA Today* and the *Indy Star*, her company, SVC, received more than $3.5 million in state contracts from the state of Indiana. At the same time, she represented Hewlett-Packard, one of the biggest private contractors for administering that state's Medicaid program. The *Star* obtained documents showing that "the company agreed to pay Verma more than $1 million and has landed more than $500 million in state contracts during her tenure as Indiana's go-to health-care consultant."

In reporting its findings, the newspaper asked the obvious question: "Who is she working for when she advises the state on how to spend billions of dollars in Medicaid funds — Hoosier taxpayers or one of the state's largest contractors?"

As we will see in the next chapter, similar questions can be asked of Verma's boss.

* *

To understand what the Price-Verma reign at HHS mean for healthcare advocates and poor Americans, there's no better place to visit than Price's home state of Georgia.

There, health care advocates are bracing for the arrival of an Indiana-style "waiver." In Atlanta, conservative lawmakers and groups are preparing a model for Medicaid expansion "the Georgia Way." The state Chamber of Commerce is leading the attempt to copy the "Indiana Way," and has helped produce a waiver application that includes work requirements, cost sharing, and year-long "lockouts" for failure to pay in to private accounts.

"Tom Price and Seema Verma want Medicaid patients to have more 'skin in the game'," said Laura Harker, a policy analyst at the Georgia Budget & Policy Institute.

"A lot of things that weren't possible under Obama are back on the table," she says. "This includes things that are often barriers to coverage for poor people, like premiums and deductibles. If you don't have a lot of money, then putting money into the accounts every month is difficult. In

Indiana, people dropped coverage or were locked out of coverage after missing one or two payments."

Harker says Georgia conservatives see Mike Pence's governorship as a role model for innovation in Medicaid, and expect the Georgia waiver to include efforts to reduce Medicaid rolls first trial ballooned under his governorship. These include drastic cuts in outreach and advertising. "A lot of people who have never had insurance before don't have information, so one way to limit participation is by limiting education and outreach," she said.

In Georgia, conservatives discuss the waiver in language suggesting concern for the poor and cash-strapped rural hospitals. But the policy outcomes tell a different story. Nowhere have penalties and cash fees been shown to reduce ER visits. But progressive experiments in Democratic-controlled states have found success in the other direction.

"In Washington State, there are successful programs to get people to their appointments and help people manage their care before they end up in the emergency room," says Harker.

Of course, Tom Price and Seema Verma have no interest in such programs, however effective they may be. They'd rather "prepare" people for "the market" — all while raking in a shit ton of money for their trouble.

Chapter Five
The Politics of Profit

On November 7, one day before the 2016 election, Tom Price addressed an industry conference called Medtrade in his home city of Atlanta. High on his list of topics was a new bidding system devised by CMS to lower Medicare costs. It involved changing the reimbursement calculus for products grouped under the term "homecare" — everything from bedpans and walkers to expensive tech like respiratory devices and chair lifts. The companies who sell these products do a heavy business with the government through Medicare. Needless to say, their trade association, the American Association for Homecare, was not happy with the CMS plan to start bargaining harder.

Neither was Tom Price. He assured the group that he shared their pain and their worry. He spoke of his plans to delay the bidding system during the remainder of the lame duck session and into the new administration. (It's doubtful he had much confidence he would be part of that administration.) He promised to lobby and educate his colleagues on the need to scrap the CMS competitive bidding program, and keep the old "market pricing approach." This approach, much preferred by industry, reflected what Price described as the more "patient-centered priorities" of people like himself and the gathered businessmen.

"The charge [of CMS] is different than yours and mine," Price said. "Your charge is to care for people. Their charge is to make the numbers add up." He added, "It's just so sad."

When it was all over, the trade association presented Price with an award. To complete the event as a microcosm of everything wrong with Tom Price, it would also hold a fundraiser for the Congressman, who had almost certainly invested in its member companies.

Upon taking the helm at HHS, Price would be forced to divest from companies like the ones in the American Association for Homecare. And PhRMA. And AHIP (the insurance association.) All told, his ascension to HHS required his selling some 40 stocks related to the healthcare industry.

By the time he made these divestments, it was too late for Tom Price to convince anyone his political and business careers bloomed from a "charge to care for people."[9]   The information unearthed between his speech to the Medtrade conference and his confirmation would forever brand him as one of the most corrupt heads of a major department in modern times. He is absolutely the most corrupt head of HHS.

Price's disclosure records show that he had traded $300,000 in healthcare-related stocks shares while serving on the health subcommittee of the House Ways and Means Committee. Kaiser Health News led the charge in putting this number in context of his government dealings, of which his lobbying for the Homecare industry was typical.

As Kaiser summarized in a January article, "Price has been a go-to congressman, a review of his records show, for medical special interests hotly sparring with regulators or facing budget cuts." In reviewing a decade of Price's communications with government health agencies, the organization found Price had "actively lobbied on FDA and other regulations that could impact companies in which he held a financial stake, as well as on issues that affected his campaign donors." This included no fewer than 38 letters to the FDA on behalf of his benefactors and personal investments.

Another report by Kaiser details just how brazen his behavior could be. He continued trading medical industry stocks even as the Securities and Exchange Commission investigated Brian Sutter, a Republican staffer on the Ways and Means Committee, for trading on inside information related to the Committee's work. (No charges were brought against Sutter, who now works as a lobbyist for Fortune 500 drug makers and healthcare providers.)

The following year, in 2012, President Obama signed a law intended to curb insider trading by members of Congress. It was called the Stop Trading on Congressional Knowledge Act. As if to show the world what he

---

[9] Price's first official brush with an ethics scandal came following the revelation that, on December 10, 2009, a day before he cast a "no" vote on Dodd-Frank, Price had hosted a $2,500 fundraising lunch at the Capitol Hill Club for banking and finance lobbyists. The day's haul of $29,000 came from the very people standing to benefit from the defeat of Dodd-Frank. When the House Office of Congressional Ethics launched a preliminary investigation, Price said their concerns were "without any merit whatsoever." It's true Price didn't need any further incentive to oppose Dodd-Frank — and a 2011 ruling by the House ethics committee that found no connection between fundraising by Price his vote — but it made clear he did not care about appearances. It was a brazenness that would later cast a shadow over his hearings.

thought of the law, Price chose that year to end a yearlong hiatus trading health care stocks. Although his profile and power had never been greater, there would be no blind trust for him, no turn toward mutual funds for the sake of ethics or appearances.

Tom Price clearly enjoys trading stocks; indeed, it may be his one true joy in life. According to Kaiser's analysis, these trades often come at curious times:

In 2012, disclosure records show Price sold stock in several drug firms, including more than $110,000 worth of Amgen stock. Amgen's stock price had steadily climbed out of a recession-level slump, but Price's sale came a few weeks before the company pleaded guilty to illegally marketing an anemia drug.... Along with investments in technology, financial services and retail stocks, he also bought and sold stock in companies that could be impacted by actions of his subcommittee, which has a role in determining rates the government pays under the Medicare program....

The list of Price's pre-HHS investments was a long one, heavy on drug companies including Incyte, Jazz Pharmaceuticals, Onyx Pharmaceuticals, CVS, Amgen, Eli Lilly, Pfizer, Biogen and Bristol-Myers Squibb. Around the time of the SEC investigation, he also bought stakes in major insurer Aetna and its medical records and billing subsidiary, Athenahealth.

While in Congress, he had at least one finger in every medical industry pie.

These investments were possible thanks to a House rule that allows for such investments so long as they are under $15,000. So Price kept his betting around this number. But small numbers can become big numbers, if added up or multiplied. This is especially true if the calculator is savvy, powerful, and shameless.

Sure enough, the day before his first confirmation hearing, *Time* magazine reported that Price had recently made six $15,000 investments in drug makers just as he embarked on a political campaign to help those very companies. It was the kind of dual-track effort that made him so valuable to industry: one in Congress, one in public, both aimed to block a CMS regulation to reduce the cut doctors made on prescribing certain expensive (and often unnecessary) cancer and arthritis drugs. This would also, of course, reduce the drug industry's ability to incentivize these prescriptions.

Price threw everything he had into helping defeat the CMS plan, called the Medicare Part B Drug Payment Model. Sources told *Time* the successful beat-back "was largely a result of the legislative and lobbying effort by the pharmaceutical industry and members of Congress."

Price, it turned out, had his fingerprints on both sides of this pincer attack. An investigation by ProPublica found the Pharma lobbyists working Congress were often products of the Congressional Office of Tom Price. Price's former chief of staff, Matt McGinley, and a former Price aide, Keagan Lenihan, lobbied Congress during the Part B fight on behalf of

Amgen and McKesson, respectively.

In February of 2017, Lenihan rejoined her old boss at HHS as his senior advisor. She took from McKesson a deeper understanding of the "dangers" of government regulation of prescription incentivizing. One month prior to reuniting with Price, her company submitted to a record settlement with the Department of Justice for failing "to detect and report suspicious orders of [oxycodone and hydrocodone] in several states."

There is no better symbol of the problems of the "free-market" in medicine than the national opioid epidemic. Drug-makers skewed perceptions of the science around opioids and addiction, lied about the potency of the new painkillers, incentivize their over-prescription, and then made a fortune as Medicaid picked up the tab on a spiraling national crisis. All the while, industry lobbyists fought off regulations and attempts to reduce drug costs.

For its exploitation of the opioid crisis, McKesson received a suspension of its license to sell controlled substances and was levied with a civil fine of $150 million.

McKesson's in-house general counsel, John Saia, argued that the company should not be held accountable for the orders placed by shady doctors and pharmacies in the most famous heroin zip codes of West Virginia and Ohio. "The two roles that interface directly with the patient— the doctors who write the prescriptions and the pharmacists who fill them—are in a better position to identify and prevent abuse and diversion of potentially addictive controlled substance," said Saia in a company statement.

If that sounds familiar, it's because it is the industrial drug dealer's version of Tom Price's go-to talking-point homily about the dyadic "patient-doctor relationship." The McKesson version adds a small-town pharmacist to the picture, but hides the same politics, and uses the same ruse. In both frames, the government should stay out of the picture — even when it's picking up the bill — because the other players have the best intentions and there are, of course, no powerful corporate actors in the drama lurking behind the scenes. There is no pharmaceutical company pushing and billing for the drugs. There are no stockholders like Tom Price reaping rewards. And even if there are, in no way are they stained with the blood of 50,000 overdoses in the year Price was nominated to run HHS.[10]

* *

During his confirmation hearings, Price feigned shock when Democratic senators raised the issue of his stock purchases and coterminous actions on behalf of those companies. His broker at Morgan Stanley, Price maintained, handled all of these transactions on her own initiative, independently of him. He knew nothing.

His claims of ignorance extended to every case raised during the hearings, such as his work on behalf of drug makers who faced the prospect of a slightly higher tax bill. The *Wall Street Journal* reports that in June of 2016, Price introduced a (failed) bill to make everlasting a tax emption for companies producing drugs in Puerto Rico. The companies just happened to include several companies in which Price had recently invested, including Eli Lilly, Bristol Myers Squibb, and Amgen.[11]

There was one story, however, that Price was unable to shake with coy claims of ignorance and smarmy reminders about the technicalities of Congressional rules.

This was the story of Innate Immunotherapeutics.

* *

The story begins in August of 2016, when Price discussed a hot little

---

[10] It appears Price has not learned much about the opioid crisis in recent years, despite being surrounded by revolving-door staffers from Big Pharma. In May, Price shocked the medical world by dismissing methadone and buprenorphine, widely used to help heroin addicts stay off junk and away from needles, as simply "substituting one opioid for another." More than 700 addiction specialists signed a letter to the HHS Secretary in an attempt to educate him on the research showing the drugs' efficacy in reducing the chance of relapse and keeping patients inside a broader treatment framework.

[11] As an industry, Pharma has it pretty good. Pharmaceutical Drug makers pay an aggregate effective tax rate of less than 20 percent — 30 percent less than engineering and construction firms, 20 percent less than Education companies, and ten points below the average across all sectors of the economy.

private offering with his friend and GOP colleague on the Ways and Means Committee, New York's Chris Collins. Innate, a boutique biotech firm incorporated in Australia, was looking to raise money. Price had already bought small chunks of Innate on three occasions the previous year. But this time was different. The firm was looking for an infusion to accelerate the timeline on its goal of a big buyout. The company's hopes rested on its only research effort within sight of approval and production: an experimental multiple sclerosis drug called MIS416.

Collins and Price were among the beneficiaries of a direct offering by the company that allowed 20 "sophisticated" U.S. investors to buy chunks of the company at a 12 percent discount. On August 31, Price purchased shares in the company worth between $50,000 to $100,000, according to his disclosure forms. Collins, whose family already owed a fifth of the company's stock, bought $720,000.

Price would turn a large and quick profit on these shares, but may wish he'd turned down the offer. A steady stream of reporting by a dozen news organizations — led by Kaiser, ProPublica, and Rewire — would flesh out the peculiarities of Price's purchase and provide heavy grist for his critics through the confirmation process.

Because of the size and globally unique profit potential of the U.S. drug market — a potential that owes much to the distorting, pro-corporate policies Price has built his career on — Innate's strategy was centered on winning quick approval by U.S. regulatory bodies. Specifically, it needed FDA approval for MIS416 as an "investigational new drug" to increase its chances of a billion-dollar buyout.

The company's CEO, Michael Quinn, already possessed a tarnished reputation from his management of previous biotech startups that crashed on FDA regulatory shoals.[12] He was determined to avoid another disaster. Quinn understood from experience the importance of having friends and a footprint in Washington.

Whatever becomes of Innate's MS drug and Michael Quinn's buyout dreams, Tom Price made out very well on what a hundred headlines have since called his "sweetheart deal" with Innate. According to a report in Dow Jones Newswire, Price sold his shares upon becoming health secretary

---

[12] According to a report in Rewire by Sharona Coutts, Quinn's previous company, QRxPharma, was the subject of a class action lawsuit filed in Australia by shareholders claiming that company executives raised tens of millions of dollars without disclosing a series of setbacks with the FDA — and thus the high-probability that its drugs would never be approved. Quinn would accidentally include the Rewire reporter on an internal email chain in which he calls her a "scumbag."

at a $225,000 profit.

The relationship between Tom Price's FDA and Innate is a matter of speculation. A matter of record is Price's actions on behalf of a medical device maker that he invested in late in his Congressional career: Zimmer Biomet.

* *

Before becoming wealthy as a medical entrepreneur and investor, Tom Price made a good living as an orthopedic surgeon. As do all orthopedic surgeons, his practice benefited greatly from Medicare, a program he would have opposed with all his might had he been in politics when it was passed in 1965. Forty-eight million seniors owe their health security to Medicare, with joint replacements making up the largest number of that group's inpatient surgeries.

Had Price satisfied himself with the millions his practice billed to Medicare over the decades, he might have avoided one of the biggest controversies that will forever be associated with his name. But in March of 2016, he decided to cut himself in on the other side of the business. That month, he made one of his $15,000 buys in a leading producer of orthopedic implants — mostly knees, hip bones and joints — then used the power of his office to increase the company's bottom line. And he did this in a very stupid way.

The company, Zimmer Biomet, was not unknown to Price. The doctors at Resurgens, his company, used its products; its PAC supported his campaigns.

Around the time of his stock purchase, Price found himself in a position to help himself and his political backers. Not for the first time, the "problem" was regulatory shenanigans cooked up by the budget-obsessed bureaucrats at CMS' Innovation Center. Just as they had attempted to reduce drug prices and regulate dangerous prescriptions, now they were on the cusp of instituting a pilot project to reduce costs and improve quality on orthopedic implants. It hit home for Price in every way. His shares in the company were the least of it.

The CMS program was called Comprehensive Care for Joint Replacement. The gist of it was a payment system that linked, or "bundled," payments and quality measurement, thus fulfilling CMS's twin mission of improving care and reducing costs. But what's good for patients and Medicare budgets can be bad for corporate profits. Once again, Price flew into action on behalf of a "constituent" that also happened to be a member of his bulging portfolio of health industry stocks.

Shortly before the new CMS payment model was scheduled to go into effect, Price introduced a bill, the HIP Act, to "delay and suspend" the new system. The bill, like most legislation Price sponsored, went nowhere. Still, Price pushed on. In September, with a chunk of Zimmer Biomet still sitting in his portfolio, he sent a letter to CMS assailing the Joint Replacement pilot program for violating the patient-doctor relationship. He took the opportunity to register his ideological opposition to very the existence of the CMS Innovation Center. The policy lab, he wrote, "exceeded its authority (and) failed to engage stakeholders" and should "cease all current and future planned mandatory initiatives."

If Tom Price hates anything, it is initiatives intended to save the government money and help people. His HIP Act would have defunded a little but landmark piece of the ACA known as the Prevention and Public Health Trust Fund. The first-ever funding stream aimed at improving overall public health through national investments, the Fund was also tasked with restraining healthcare costs. In its six years of existence, it had supported research and outreach programs aimed at reducing major causes of preventable death and disability, and improving the government's ability to detect and respond to new threats to public health.

To most people, this Fund sounds like a pretty good thing. For Price, it is a painful corn requiring immediate excision. Why? Aside from ideology, Price was also doing the bidding of his Big Tobacco "constituents." Over the years, the cigarette industry has contributed tens of thousands of dollars to his campaigns, rewarding his service as one of the most loyal and dogged defenders of the industry's right to kill hundreds of thousands of Americans without the threat of regulation.

* *

The coda to this brief review of the stink around Tom Price predates the Innate Immunotherapeautics and Zimmer Biomet episodes. It also finds Price on the other side of a CMS reform proposal.

The year was 2013. CMS had proposed changes to the government's billing system for skin grafts and other wound treatment products. The new rules were aimed at reducing waste, but were structured in such a way that doctors who used certain products were reimbursed at a higher rate. Among the companies in line to see increased Medicare payouts was MiMedx, a Georgia-based company that did heavy business with VA hospitals and Medicare.

Usually, Price would lambast the CMS effort as a case of government overreach and meddling — of Uncle Sam "picking winners and losers." But this time, the winner was a "constituent." As the *Daily Beast* reported, Price led a group of lawmakers in writing a letter to CMS in support of the rule change, even singling out for praise a MiMedx product called EpiFix. The rule change went into effect. Six months later, MiMedx's PAC started giving

Tom Price money. It was his biggest donor during his final year in Congress.[13]

The rule change advocated by Price didn't just increase MiMedx profits; it doubled them. A year later, the company was aggressively courting investors with a rosy picture of its position in a wounded care market with eight-figure growth estimates. Lost amid the company and investor celebrations over booming business was the backstory of its trade with the VA, where government doctors patched the wounds of foreign wars supported with gusto by MiMedx CEO Parker Petit and Congressman Tom Price.

---

[13] Much of that money may have been strong-armed from MiMedx employs by its Republican stalwart CEO, Parker H. Petit. Kaiser later reported that in 2013 Petit sent managers an email demanding donations to a political action committee supportive of GOP candidates and causes. "I'm going to ask one more time for our field management to send something to our PAC. And, IMMEDIATELY," said the email. "We have PAC business to transact, and we need at least 50 donors to do so." At the time, according to Kaiser, Petit was lobbying the FDA to alter its regulation of MiMedx, after a critical FDA review of its products resulted in weakened shares and settlements with angry stockholders. In Washington, Petit's main ally in challenging the FDA was Johnny Isakson, the Georgia senator whose House seat Price inherited, and who would introduce him at his first HHS confirmation hearing.

ABOUT THE AUTHOR

Alexander Zaitchik is a freelance journalist whose writing has appeared in The Nation, The New Republic, Rolling Stone, Mother Jones, Vice, The Guardian, and many other publications. He is the author of two books, *Common Nonsense: Glenn Beck and the Triumph of Ignorance*, and *The Gilded Rage: A Wild Ride Through Donald Trump's America*. He lives in New Orleans.

Made in the USA
San Bernardino, CA
30 June 2017